Slim Goodbody's Life Skills 101

HAVE YOU HEARD?

Active Listening

CRABTREE
Publishing Company
www.crabtreebooks.com

Crabtree Publishing Company
www.crabtreebooks.com

Series Development, Writing, and Packaging:
John Burstein, Slim Goodbody Corp.

Editors:
Reagan Miller, Valerie Weber, and Mark Sachner,
   Water Buffalo Books

Editorial director:
Kathy Middleton

Production coordinator:
Kenneth Wright

Prepress technicians:
Kenneth Wright

Designer: Tammy West, Westgraphix LLC.

Photos: Chris Pinchback, Pinchback Photography

"Slim Goodbody" and Pinchback photos, copyright,
© Slim Goodbody

"Slim Goodbody" and "Slim Goodbody's Life
Skills 101" are registered trademarks of the Slim
Goodbody Corp.

Photo credits:
iStockPhotos: p. 4 (top), 6 (right), 9 (top), 23 (top),
   27 (top)
Shutterstock: p. 5 (bottom), 6 (left), 7 (top),
   12 (top), 25 (bottom), 29 (bottom)
© Slim Goodbody: p. 1, 4 (bottom), 5 (top),
   7 (bottom), 8 (all), 9 (bottom), 10, 11 (all),
   12 (bottom), 13, 14 (all), 15, 16 (all), 17 (bottom),
   18 (all), 19 (all), 20, 21, 22, 23 (bottom), 24, 25 (top),
   26, 27 (bottom), 28, 29 (top)

Acknowledgements:
The author would like to thank the following
children for all their help in this project: Stephanie
Bartlett , Sarah Booth, Christine Burstein, Lucas
Burstein, Olivia Davis, Eleni Fernald, Kylie Fong,
Tristan Fong, Colby Hill, Carrie Laurita, Ginny
Laurita, Henry Laurita, Louis Laurita, Nathan
Levig, Havana Lyman, Renaissance Lyman,
Andrew McBride, Lulu McClure, Yanmei
McElhaney, Amanda Mirabile, Esme Power, Emily
Pratt, Andrew Smith, Dylan Smith, Mary Wells

Library and Archives Canada Cataloguing in Publication

Burstein, John
       Have you heard? : active listening / John Burstein.

(Slim Goodbody's life skills 101)
Includes index.
ISBN 978-0-7787-4790-1 (bound).--ISBN 978-0-7787-4806-9 (pbk.)

       1. Listening--Juvenile literature. I. Title. II. Title: Active listening.
III. Series: Burstein, John. Slim Goodbody's life skills 101.

BF323.L5B87 2010   j153.6'8   C2009-903571-5

Library of Congress Cataloging-in-Publication Data

Burstein, John.
   Have you heard? Active listening / John Burstein.
       p. cm. -- (Slim Goodbody's life skills 101)
   Includes index.
   ISBN 978-0-7787-4806-9 (pbk. : alk. paper) -- ISBN 978-0-7787-4790-1 (reinforced
library binding : alk. paper)
   1. Listening--Juvenile literature. I. Title.
   BF323.L5B88 2010
   153.6'8--dc22

                                                                    2009022851

Crabtree Publishing Company

Published in Canada
Crabtree Publishing
616 Welland Ave.
St. Catharines, Ontario
L2M 5V6

Published in the United States
Crabtree Publishing
PMB16A
350 Fifth Ave., Suite 3308
New York, NY 10118

Published in the United Kingdom
Crabtree Publishing
White Cross Mills
High Town, Lancaster
LA1 4XS

Published in Australia
Crabtree Publishing
386 Mt. Alexander Rd.
Ascot Vale (Melbourne)
VIC 3032

CONTENTS

Words in **bold** are defined
in the glossary on page 30.

LISTEN HERE!

Patty was shocked. She was a good student and usually made all A's and B's. Not this time. Her history quiz was marked C-! How could this have happened?

She went to her teacher and said, "Excuse me, Mr. Raines. I have a question."

"Sure, Patty, what is it?" replied her teacher.

"How did I get such a bad mark on the quiz? I studied hard, and I knew the answers to your questions," Patty said.

"Patty, you didn't answer my question at all," said her teacher.

Patty was confused. "But I gave a lot of reasons why the first Thanksgiving was important to the Pilgrims."

"That wasn't the question I asked," explained Mr. Raines. "I asked you to write about why the first Thanksgiving was important to the Native Americans!"

"Are you sure?" asked Patty with surprise.

"Well, that's the question all the other kids answered." Mr. Raines said kindly.

Patty gulped. "Guess I didn't listen very well, did I?"

Mr. Raines smiled, "I guess not, but I'm sure you will next time."

Hi. My name is Slim Goodbody.

The story you just read is not unusual. Many people make mistakes because they do not know how to listen well. Luckily, you can improve your listening ability. You can learn a terrific skill called active listening.

Active listening will help you

• do better in school;

• get along better with your friends;

• make family meal times more interesting.

Want to find out more? Read on!

HERE'S HOW YOU HEAR

Before you can understand active listening, you need to learn how hearing works.

Sound begins with **vibrations**. When something vibrates, it moves back and forth. For example, when you pluck guitar strings, they vibrate. As the strings vibrate, they move the nearby **atoms** in the air. These atoms cause other atoms to vibrate. The vibrations form a sound wave that moves out from the strings.

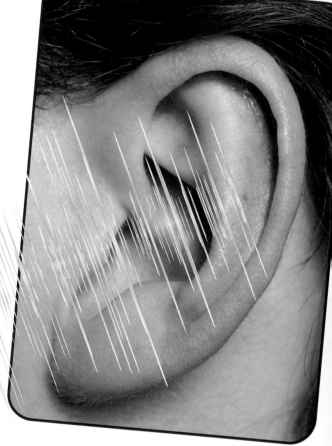

An image might help you understand this. Imagine you dropped a stone into a pool of water. The stone creates a ripple that moves out from where the stone fell. A sound wave moves out from its source in the same way.

1. The sound wave reaches your outer ear.

5. The vibration moves along to the inner ear. Special hearing **nerves** send the sound messages to your brain.

2. The sound wave enters a short **passageway** leading to your **eardrum**.

3. The sound wave makes your eardrum vibrate.

4. The eardrum is connected to three small bones in the middle ear. These small bones also start vibrating.

Once your brain receives the message, your brain decides whether you should **respond** to the sound. For example, if the sound is a fire alarm, you need to leave the building. If it's the sound of a radio playing in the next room, you can safely ignore it."

Your Brilliant Brain

You have a brilliant brain. Hearing, however, is only one of the senses it must deal with. Your brain is also getting information from your eyes, nose, mouth, and skin. Information pours in every second. Your brain simply can't focus on all of it at one time. If you decide that what you are hearing is very important, your brain will focus on that. Focusing is the first step toward active listening.

ARE YOU LISTENING OR JUST HEARING?

There is a big difference between hearing and listening. Hearing takes no work. Sounds simply enter your ear. Listening takes **energy**. You have to use your brain to focus on the sounds you are hearing.

Musical Chairs

Remember playing a game called Musical Chairs? As music played, you and your friends marched around a group of chairs. There's always one less chair than the number of players. When the music stopped, you rushed to sit down to make sure you got a seat. Not only did you hear the music, but you listened as well.

Remember the last time that you were at the mall or in a store? Music was probably playing over a speaker, but you hardly noticed. You could hear the music, but you weren't really listening.

Surround Sound

At this very moment, you are probably surrounded by sounds. Even in a quiet library, you can still hear pages turning, books closing, chairs scraping against the floor, and people whispering.

Try This: Experiment #1

Stop reading, and really listen to the sounds around you. Do you notice a change in how your mind begins to work? You begin to focus. You use more energy. You have shifted from hearing to active listening.

SPEED LIMITS

When people talk to you, your goal should be to listen. Reaching that goal is not as easy as it sounds. Even if you decide to listen to what someone is saying, you may still miss a lot. One of the reasons for this is brain speed. Your brilliant brain thinks too fast!

You can think four times faster than you can speak. Let me explain. Suppose someone speaks to you at a speed of 600 to 750 words a minute. Your brain can keep up with the words being spoken and understand what was said. Human beings, however, can't speak this fast. Most of us talk at a speed of 150 to 175 words per minute. So your brain has time for listening plus extra time as well.

Brain Power

This extra time can help you understand what the person is saying. It can also get in the way of understanding. Instead of listening, you might use the extra time to think about something else, perhaps what you want to do later; think about what you want to say when the speaker stops; think about something you just noticed, for example, a friend walking past.

Sometimes you think that you already know what a person will say. After the first few sentences, you stop listening and start focusing on other things. If you are not a mind reader, however, you might be making a big mistake.

Try This: Experiment #2

Find a book, and read a page out loud as fast as you can. Ask a friend to time you for one minute. Now, go back and count how many words you read. Think about how you talk in everyday life. What do you think your normal talking speed is?

LISTEN AND LEARN

People learn by listening. Here's a fact you might find amazing at first:

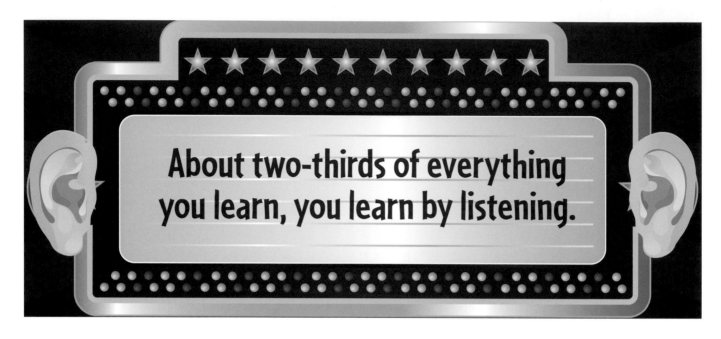

About two-thirds of everything you learn, you learn by listening.

Think about it, though. You learn to talk by listening to the words spoken by your parents, older brothers and sisters, and other people around you.

Listening allows you

- to get useful information;
- to solve problems;
- to avoid confusion;
- to understand what other people think;
- to understand how people feel;
- to share interests with others.

Why People Talk

Sometimes people talk because they're bored and want something to do. Sometimes they're lonely and just want company. Most of the time, however, people talk for one or more of the following reasons:

to explain something;

to ask for something;

to share thoughts;

to share feelings.

When people talk, they are sending a message. Their message contains information of some kind. They want this information to be received by a listener. The goal of active listening is to receive someone's message and understand it correctly. Let's learn how to do it!

ATTENTION, PLEASE!

The first step to becoming a good active listener is to pay attention. When someone is speaking, stay completely focused on what he or she is saying. Don't allow your mind to drift off.

Learning to pay attention takes practice. If you notice your mind drifting off while someone speaks, gently bring your attention back to the speaker.

The Eyes Have It

To help you pay attention, use your eyes. Keep looking at the speaker the whole time he talks. If you look around the room, you can easily get interested in something else. You can lose track of what he is saying.

Looking at someone also shows that you're interested. Your interest helps the other person feel comfortable sharing his thoughts.

Imagine

Imagine you were having a conversation with a friend. What if your friend started to do some of the following?

• Looking in the other direction

• Glancing at her watch or the clock

• Doodling on a piece of paper

• Smiling or waving to other people

• Reading a book or magazine

How would you feel? Would you think that your friend was paying attention and listening? Would you think she cared about what you were saying? Would you wonder if it was worth speaking more? Try to be the kind of listener you would want if you were speaking.

Eye Freeze

When you are listening to someone, do not keep your eyes frozen in place. In other words, don't stare. Your **gaze** should be friendly and open. You can look at the speaker's face as a whole. Then look in his eyes for a moment or two. Shift your gaze to the person's hands and then back to his face.

   Don't move your eyes around too much. You don't want to look wild and strange!

Try This: Experiment #3

Practice looking at a friend for one minute. For the first 30 seconds, try staring. For the next 30 seconds, use a friendly, open gaze. See if you can feel the difference between these two ways of looking. Ask your friend if she could notice the difference as well.

MIND CLUTTER

You won't be able to pay complete attention if you don't control your thinking. If your brain gets cluttered with your own thoughts, there won't be room to let in what the other person has to say. Mind clutter might include

- figuring out what you want to say when the speaker stops talking;
- remembering what happened earlier in the day;
- daydreaming about what you'll be doing later;
- thinking about a story you're working on in English class.

Control the Clutter

To become a good active listener, control your thinking. Set aside cluttering thoughts and **concentrate** on what the speaker is saying. If you're finding it hard to concentrate on what someone is saying, try one of the following **strategies**:

control the clutter

ECHO Repeat the speaker's words silently as he says them. Pretend you hear an echo in your mind. Once you are paying full attention again, you can stop the echo.

 **MAGNIFY** Imagine you are looking at the speaker through a magnifying glass. In your imagination, you are making him bigger and more important. As you do this, your attention to what he is saying should increase. You'll be less likely to pay attention to movements around you, too.

BREATHE Take a deep breath and imagine you are breathing in the speaker's words along with the air.

 **TURN OFF** When thoughts come, imagine they are playing on an inner radio. Imagine pushing a button and shutting the radio off.

BLOCK OUT Build an **imaginary** mental wall to block thoughts. Don't allow your thoughts to get over, under, or around that wall.

BLOCK OUT

Keep Practicing

Keep practicing. If your own thoughts keep popping up, don't fight them. As soon as you realize you're not listening, use one of these strategies to bring your attention back to the speaker.

BODY LANGUAGE

Using and understanding **body language** is an **essential** part of active listening.

Body language allows people to **communicate** without using words. Think about it. When you are listening to someone, you need to keep silent. At the same time, you need to let that person know you are interested in what he's saying! Body language to the rescue!

Express Yourself

You can communicate by doing these things.

1. Lean forward slightly as the person talks. This shows you are interested in what she has to say.

2. Nod every once in a while. This shows you are paying attention and understand what is being said.

3. Smile every once in a while. This shows you are enjoying yourself.

Using body language also reminds you to pay attention and not let your mind wander.

Look and Learn

You can learn a lot by watching someone's body language. Body language can help you understand how the speaker feels about what he is saying. For example, if the speaker is leaning forward a bit, you know he likes what he is talking about. If he is looking down or away, he may be ashamed or upset. If his hands are shaking, he might be feeling a little nervous or scared.

When you practice active listening, you can discover what a person is thinking *and* feeling. Knowing both allows you to better understand the full meaning of the message being sent.

Try This: Experiment #4

Imagine you can't talk, but you still want to communicate with your classmates. How would you communicate the following using body language?

- "Hello!" • "I'm shocked." • "I'm sad."
 "I don't know." • "I'm mad." • "I'm tired." • "I'm bored."

This experiment should help you realize how much your body language communicates to others even when you aren't saying a word.

FRIENDLY PHRASES

When someone is talking, she will pause from time to time. She may be taking a breath or thinking for a moment about what she wants to say next. At these points, you can help keep the conversation going with a short, friendly phrase. For example:

"Uh huh"

"Um-hmm"

"I see"

"That's interesting"

"Really?"

"Yes"

"Go on"

You are not using friendly phrases to agree with the person. You are simply showing that you are listening. The goal of using friendly phrases is to give the speaker the **self-confidence** to keep talking.

Train Tracks

Think of a person's words as a train moving down a track. Imagine that every once in a while, there's a break in the track. Friendly phrases fill in that break. They help keep the word train moving along smoothly.

As the word train moves down the tracks, here are some things to keep in mind:

- Don't **interrupt** and try to put your word train on the track instead. Don't say something like, "The same thing happened to me. Let me tell you about it."

- Don't switch the train's direction by asking a lot of questions. Don't ask a question such as, "Why would you want to do that?"

- Don't try to control someone's train by giving advice when you are not asked for it. One example might be, "You should not have done that. Here is what you should have done."

Sound of Silence

Don't be afraid of silence. When someone is speaking to you, every moment cannot be filled with words. Use the silences to think about what the person is saying and feeling.

REFLECTING

Even when you practice all these steps, you can still get the message wrong. While you listen to someone speak, you think you understand what she means. Later on, however, you discover that you were wrong.

To keep this from happening, active listeners use a special tool called reflecting. Reflecting means that you repeat back what the speaker has just said, but you do it in your own words. You also make the information into a question. Here's an example of how reflecting works.

Suppose your friend was upset and said,

> "I got really mad when you were playing a game with Kayla!"

Reflecting her statement back, you might ask,

> "Are you saying you don't want me to play with Kayla?"

That might be what your friend means, but it might not. She might say,

> "No, that's not what I mean. I want to be a part of your game. I like Kayla too."

Getting Clear

Reflecting doesn't mean that you're agreeing with your friend. You're just trying to get a clearer understanding of what she is trying to communicate. Reflecting lets your friend find out whether you really understood her or not. If you didn't, she can explain some more. Reflecting can also help you discover if you've drifted off during the conversation.

Reflecting Phrases

You can begin reflecting with one of these phrases:

- "If I understand, you just said . . ."
- "Are you saying . . . ?"
- "Do you mean . . . ?"
- "Is this what you mean . . . ?"
- "What I think I'm hearing is. . . . Is that correct?"

WAIT YOUR TURN

Active listeners wait until a person is done speaking before they start talking. Waiting is not only polite, it is also smart. Remember, the point of active listening is to understand what is being said. When someone is in the middle of speaking his mind, you can't be sure what he wants to say until he has finished saying it. You have no way to know the whole story unless you wait for the end.

You may disagree with the person. You may have something important to add to what he has said. You just need to wait your turn to share your thoughts. When you are speaking, the other person has the chance to listen actively to you.

Speak Up

When your turn comes,

- speak your thoughts respectfully;

- be open and honest;

- remember your body language;

- treat the other person as you would like to be treated.

When you are finished speaking, the other person can respond to you. Your conversation will flow back and forth until each one says what they want to.

Later On

After your conversation is over and you have a little time alone, ask yourself these questions:

- What did I learn from him?

- What did I learn about him?

- Did I truly understand what he was talking about?

- If I didn't understand something, did I ask for more information?

- How can I improve my next conversation?

HARD LISTENING

When you're arguing with someone, active listening is really important. It's also really hard, because your emotions get stirred up. If you think someone is **criticizing** you, you usually start feeling hurt or angry. These are powerful feelings. They can sweep you up and make you forget about active listening.
When you're hurt or angry, it's hard

- to keep your thoughts under control;
- not to interrupt;
- not to focus on what you want to say back;
- not to want to win the argument;
- to let the other person finish speaking.

Letting the other person finish speaking lets you know what the real problem is before you answer back.

Keeping Cool

If you allow your angry feelings to rule, chances are the argument will get worse. When you are in an argument, try to keep cool.

• Keep your body language open. Don't start frowning, crossing your arms, or rolling your eyes.

• Use friendly phrases such as, "I'm listening," and "Go on."

• Practice reflecting if you don't understand something.

• Wait for the other person to finish speaking before you answer.

• You can start by saying, "I understand your point. Will you listen to mine?"

Keep Practicing

If you practice active listening, some important things can happen. First, the other person will know that you are trying to understand what he is talking about. This knowledge will probably lessen his anger. He will be able to explain himself more clearly.

Second, there are two sides to every argument. Sometimes a person just needs to be understood before he is willing to see someone else's point of view. If both people in an argument feel understood, they can solve their differences more quickly and easily.

REMEMBER THIS

Here is a really amazing fact:

Most people only remember about one-quarter of the information they are told.

If a teacher talks for 20 minutes, most of her students only remember about five minutes of what she says. One reason people remember so little is that they don't practice active listening. They allow their minds to drift off and think of other things. They want to speak instead of listen.

Two to One

Remember that you have two ears and only one mouth. There's a good reason for that: You learn more when you listen than when you talk.

When you become an active listener, you become a much better learner. You listen to the words someone speaks and try to understand the total message being sent.

Just for Fun

Here are a few exercises you can do by yourself to practice active listening:

- When you are out walking, "tune-in" to the different "sound channels" around you. There are a lot out there—the bird channel, the insect channel, the voice channel, the traffic channel, the wind channel, the rain channel, and so on. See how many sounds you can hear in five minutes.

- Next time you're with friends, see if you can listen twice as long as you speak.

Now You Know

Now you know that with active listening you'll learn more. You will also make a better friend and get along better with others. Remember, however, that every new skill takes practice. Each day, promise yourself that you will try to hear and listen.

GLOSSARY

atoms The smallest particles in the world. Everything is made up of atoms.

body language The way a person moves or holds himself or herself that communicates to other people

communicate To give information, thoughts, or feelings to other people

concentrate To focus on something or someone; to pay attention to something or someone

criticizing Saying something bad about a person or his or her activities

eardrum The thin layer that separates the outer and middle ear and carries sound waves to the small bones in the middle ear

energy The strength or willingness to get something done

essential Absolutely necessary or very important

gaze The way you look at someone; a long, steady look

imaginary Describing something that exists only in the mind

interrupt To stop a person from speaking or moving

nerves Special cells that carry signals to and from the brain

passageway A path that something or someone can move along

respond To react, or act in return

self-confidence Trust or faith in yourself and in your powers and abilities

strategies Plans for achieving goals

vibrations Rapid motions back and forth or from side to side

BOOKS

Active Listening: Introducing Skills for Understanding (Student's Book 1) Marc Helgesen (Author), Steven Brown (Author). Cambridge University Press.

The Boy Who Loved Words. Roni Schotter (Author), Giselle Potter (Illustrator). Schwartz & Wade.

Hearing (Our Senses). Kay Woodward. Hodder Wayland.

Perk Up Your Ears: Discover Your Sense of Hearing. Vicki Cobb (Author), Cynthia Lewis (Illustrator), Vicki Cobb (Author). Millbrook Press.

Hearing (Senses and Sensors). Alvin Silverstein. 21st Century.

WEB SITES

Kidshealth
kidshealth.org/kid/htbw/ears.html
Check out this Web site for information on how your sense of hearing works.

PBS Kids
pbskids.org/itsmylife/friends/friendsfight/article3.html
On this wonderful Web site you can play games and learn more about what to do if you have a fight with a friend.

Discovery Kids
yucky.discovery.com/flash/body/yuckystuff/earwax/js.index.html
This Web site is a science education site that makes learning fun. There is plenty of information about the human body, including tips for keeping your ears healthy.

Slim Goodbody
slimgoodbody.com
Discover loads of fun and free downloads for kids, teachers, and parents.

INDEX

About the Author
John Burstein (also known as Slim Goodbody) has been entertaining and educating children for over thirty years. His programs have been broadcast on CBS, PBS, Nickelodeon, USA, and Discovery. He has won numerous awards including the Parent's Choice Award and the President's Council's Fitness Leader Award. Currently, Mr. Burstein tours the country with his multimedia live show "Bodyology." For more information, please visit **slimgoodbody.com**.

Printed in the U.S.A.— CG